Holiday Cooking for Kids!

VALENTINE'S DAY
Sweets and Treats

By Ruth Owen

WINDMILL
BOOKS

New York

Published in 2013 by Windmill Books, An Imprint of Rosen Publishing
29 East 21st Street, New York, NY 10010

First Edition

Produced for Windmill by Ruby Tuesday Books Ltd
Editor for Ruby Tuesday Books Ltd: Mark J. Sachner
US Editor: Sara Antill
Designer: Trudi Webb

Photo Credits:
Cover, 1, 3, 4–5, 6–7, 8–9, 10–11, 12–13, 14–15, 17, 18–19, 20–21, 22–23, 24–25, 26–27, 28–29, 30–31 © Shutterstock; 16 © Alamy.

Library of Congress Cataloging-in-Publication Data

Owen, Ruth, 1967–
Valentine's Day sweets and treats / by Ruth Owen.
        p. cm. — (Holiday cooking for kids!)
  Includes index.
   ISBN 978-1-4488-8080-5 (library binding) — ISBN 978-1-4488-8127-7 (pbk.) —
ISBN 978-1-4488-8133-8 (6-pack)
  1. Valentine's Day cooking—Juvenile literature. 2. Desserts—Juvenile literature. I. Title.
TX739.2.V34O94 2013
  641.5'68—dc23
                                        2012009784

Manufactured in the United States of America

CPSIA Compliance Information: Batch # B3S12WM: For Further Information contact Windmill Books, New York, New York at 1-866-478-0556

Contents

A Festival of Treats, Sweets, and Love 4

Before You Begin Cooking 6

Easy Valentine's Rocky Road 8

I Love You Cookies 12

Ti Amo Linguine! 16

Frozen Strawberry Yogurt Dessert..........................20

Red Velvet Cupcakes...24

Super Strawberry Slushies......................................28

Chocolate-Dipped Strawberries 30

Glossary, Index, and Websites 32

We don't know much about how Valentine's Day (or St. Valentine's Day), February 14, became a day to celebrate love. In fact, not just one, but several **saints** were named Valentine! According to **tradition**, one of them was **executed** by an emperor of **ancient Rome** for refusing to give up his Christian beliefs. The Church made February 14 his **feast day**.

There was no connection between that day and romance until 1382, when English poet Geoffrey Chaucer called St. Valentine's Day the "day when every bird cometh to choose his mate." Over the years, February 14 became a day when people showed their love by presenting flowers, candies, and greeting cards.

Today, we still do all these things. We also go out for special Valentine's Day meals, or we cook for our Valentines at home.

The recipes in this book give you some sweet treats to make as Valentine's gifts. There's also a dinner idea that you can make for the people you love!

Before you start cooking, check out all the tips and information on the following pages.

Before You Begin Cooking

Get Ready to Cook

- Wash your hands using soap and hot water. This will help to keep bacteria away from your food.
- Make sure the kitchen countertop and all your equipment is clean.
- Read the recipe carefully before you start cooking. If you don't understand a step, ask an adult to help you.
- Gather all the ingredients and equipment you will need.

Safety First!

It's very, very important to have an adult around whenever you do any of the following tasks in the kitchen:

1. Operating machinery or turning on kitchen appliances such as a mixer, food processor, blender, stovetop burners, or the oven.

2. Using sharp utensils, such as knives, can openers, or vegetable peelers.

3. Working with hot pots, pans, or cookie sheets.

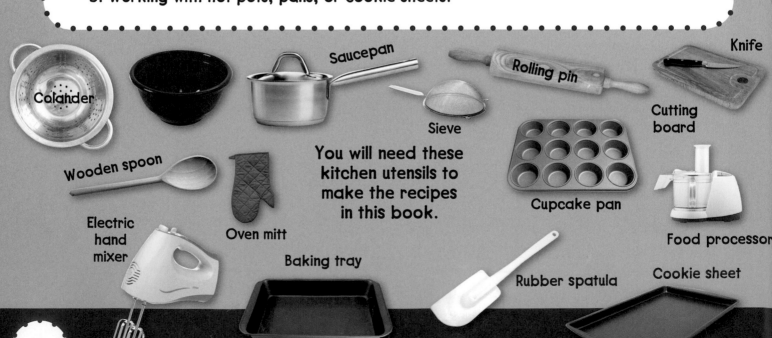

Colander

Wooden spoon

Electric hand mixer

Oven mitt

Baking tray

Saucepan

Sieve

You will need these kitchen utensils to make the recipes in this book.

Cupcake pan

Rubber spatula

Rolling pin

Knife

Cutting board

Food processor

Cookie sheet

Measuring Counts!

Measure your ingredients carefully. If you get a measurement wrong, it could affect how successful your dish turns out to be. Measuring cups and spoons are two of the most important pieces of equipment in a kitchen.

Measuring cup

Measuring Cups

Measuring cups are used to measure the volume, or amount, of liquid or dry ingredients. Measuring cups usually hold from 1 cup to 4 cups. If you have a 1-cup measuring cup, that should be fine for all the recipes in this book. Measuring cups have markings on them that show how many cups or parts of a cup you are measuring.

Measuring Spoons

Like measuring cups, measuring spoons are used to measure the volume of liquid or dry ingredients, only in smaller amounts. Measuring spoons come in sets with different spoons for teaspoons, tablespoons, and smaller parts.

Measuring spoons

Cooking Techniques

Here are some tasks that anyone who is following directions for cooking should be sure to understand.

Bringing to a boil

Heating a liquid or mixture in a saucepan on the stovetop until it is bubbling.

Simmering

First bringing a liquid or mixture to a boil, and then turning down the heat so it's just at or below the boiling point and the bubbling has nearly stopped.

Preheating

Heating the oven until it has reached the temperature required for the recipe.

All of these tasks require the use of heat, so you should be absolutely sure to have an adult around when you do them.

For hundreds of years, chocolate and love have gone hand in hand. Chocolate has long been given as a romantic gift to show love. In the 1800s, doctors even prescribed it as a cure to help people with broken hearts feel better!

Every Valentine's Day, millions of boxes of candy are purchased and given as gifts, but it's super easy to make your own. This rocky road recipe is perfect as a Valentine's gift for your parents, a friend, or that special someone whose heart you want to win!

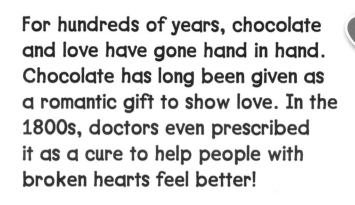

We ♥ Food!

Chocolate comes from the seeds of the cacao tree, which is native to Mexico and Central and South America. There, the history of chocolate began around 3,000 years ago. In both Mayan and Aztec cultures, cacao seeds were presented to the gods, and chocolate drinks were served during sacred ceremonies.

You will need – ingredients:

3 large dark chocolate (also known as "mildly sweet chocolate") candy bars, approximately 12 ounces (340 g) of chocolate

2 tablespoons golden syrup

1 cup mini marshmallows

1 cup of your favorite cookies broken into pieces

1 cup candied cherries (cut some in half)

2 tablespoons confectioners' sugar (for dusting)

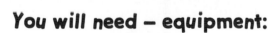

You will need – equipment:
Baking tray
Waxed paper
Medium size bowl
Rubber spatula (for stirring and spreading)
Cutting board
Knife

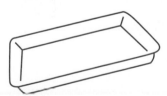

Step-by-Step:

Remember to ask an adult for help when you are using the microwave and knife.

1. Line the baking tray with waxed paper.

2. Break up the chocolate into pieces and put into a bowl.

3. Microwave for 30 seconds on high to melt the chocolate.

4. Stir the chocolate. Microwave for another 30 seconds.

5. Stir the chocolate and let the heat of the chocolate melt the lumps. If you still have lumps, microwave for 10 more seconds. Keep stirring and giving the chocolate 10-second blasts in the microwave until it is fully melted and smooth.

6. Once the chocolate is completely melted, add the other ingredients to the bowl and gently stir. Make sure you don't break up the cookie pieces too much.

7. Pour the mixture into the lined baking tray. Use the spatula to smooth out the mixture.

8. Put the baking tray into the refrigerator for a few hours, or overnight, until the rocky road mixture becomes solid.

9. Take the slab of rocky road out of the baking tray and put it on a cutting board. Carefully cut it into squares. You can make little bite-size pieces, or cut the rocky road into bigger chunks.

10. Dust with the confectioners' sugar.

I Love You Cookies

In ancient days, doctors, scientists, and poets alike thought of the heart as the center of human emotions, including love. The symbol of a heart still means "love" to most of us today. Even though it doesn't look that much like a real human heart, when we see a red heart on bumper stickers and T-shirts, or drawn on a Valentine's card, we all understand just what it means, no matter what language we speak! The recipe on these pages, for heart-shaped cookies, should be perfectly lovely for showing others just how much we really do love them!

You will need – ingredients:

1½ cups of all-purpose flour

¼ cup sugar

1 stick butter, softened

1 medium egg

¼ teaspoon baking powder

1 teaspoon vanilla extract

8 tablespoons strawberry jam

¼ cup confectioners' (powdered) sugar

1 tablespoon water

Finely shredded coconut

You will need – equipment:

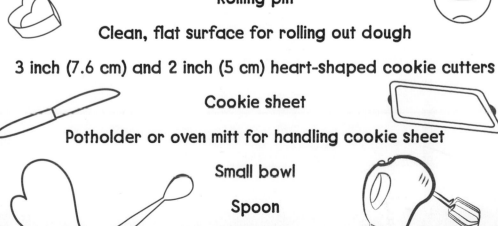

Large mixing bowl

Electric hand mixer

Plastic wrap

Rolling pin

Clean, flat surface for rolling out dough

3 inch (7.6 cm) and 2 inch (5 cm) heart-shaped cookie cutters

Cookie sheet

Potholder or oven mitt for handling cookie sheet

Small bowl

Spoon

Butter knife

13

Remember to ask an adult for help when you are using the electric hand mixer and oven.

Step-by-Step:

1. Using the electric mixer, beat the butter and sugar together until creamy in the mixing bowl, then add the egg and vanilla extract and beat until well blended.

2. Gradually add the flour and baking powder, and beat until it's just blended.

3. Shape the dough into a ball, wrap in plastic wrap, and cool in the refrigerator for an hour or in the freezer for 30 minutes.

4. Ask an adult to help you preheat the oven to 350°F (175°C).

5. Place the chilled dough on a flat, lightly floured surface and roll out until it's about ¼ inch (0.6 cm) thick.

6. For each cookie you will need to cut out two hearts using the 3 inch (7.6 cm) heart-shaped cookie cutter. Then use the 2 inch (5 cm) cookie cutter to cut a hole in one of the hearts.

Step-by-Step:

7. Place the cookies 1 inch (2.5 cm) apart on the cookie sheet and bake in the preheated oven for 10 to 12 minutes, or until lightly browned. Take out to cool.

8. While the cookies are baking, put the confectioners' sugar and water into the small bowl and mix to make a paste. If it's too wet, add a little more sugar. If it's too dry, add drops of water. The icing should be thick, but spreadable.

9. When the cookies are cooled, spread jam on one side of the cookie without the hole using a butter knife. Then sandwich a cookie with a hole on top.

10. Use the butter knife to thinly spread the white icing over the cookie with the hole. Then sprinkle on some coconut before the icing dries.

Ti Amo Linguine!

"Ti amo" is Italian for "I love you," and anyone who's ever watched the classic Disney movie *Lady and the Tramp* knows how romantic an Italian dinner can be. When the two starry-eyed dogs accidentally kiss as they swallow opposite ends of a strand of spaghetti, it's love at first bite! Here's a quick recipe for a tasty Italian dish that will put the "heart" in hearty! It can be for you and your valentine or for your Mom and Dad, or anyone else you love. Add some romance by asking an adult to help you serve it by candlelight. Also, check out the delicious dessert on page 20 that you can make to follow your pasta.

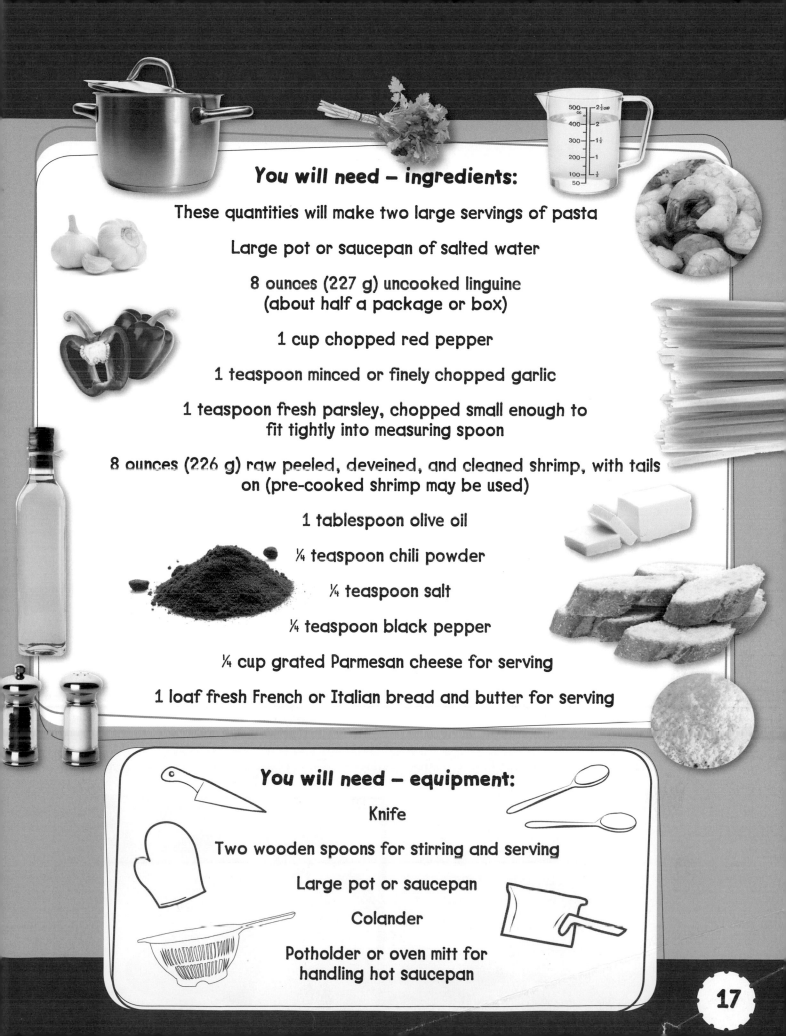

You will need – ingredients:

These quantities will make two large servings of pasta

Large pot or saucepan of salted water

8 ounces (227 g) uncooked linguine
(about half a package or box)

1 cup chopped red pepper

1 teaspoon minced or finely chopped garlic

1 teaspoon fresh parsley, chopped small enough to
fit tightly into measuring spoon

8 ounces (226 g) raw peeled, deveined, and cleaned shrimp, with tails
on (pre-cooked shrimp may be used)

1 tablespoon olive oil

¼ teaspoon chili powder

¼ teaspoon salt

¼ teaspoon black pepper

¼ cup grated Parmesan cheese for serving

1 loaf fresh French or Italian bread and butter for serving

You will need – equipment:

Knife

Two wooden spoons for stirring and serving

Large pot or saucepan

Colander

Potholder or oven mitt for
handling hot saucepan

Step-by-Step:

Raw shrimp

1. Bring the salted water to a boil over medium heat.

2. Add the linguine to the boiling water, and cook according to the directions on the package.

3. When the linguine is cooked, drain in the colander.

4. In the saucepan or pot, add the olive oil and red peppers.

5. Heat the red peppers over a low heat for about 1 minute, stirring.

6. Add the shrimp, garlic, parsley, chili powder, salt, and pepper and bring up to a medium heat, stirring frequently, until the garlic is just cooked and the shrimp begin to turn pink (about 3–4 minutes). (Note: If you are using pre-cooked shrimp, heating time for the shrimp will be much shorter. They may be added when other ingredients are nearly done being heated.)

7. Add the drained linguine to the saucepan, carefully mix all the ingredients together for a minute or two, and turn off heat.

8. Dish into individual serving bowls or into a large bowl and let everyone help themselves.

9. Serve with bread and butter and a little grated Parmesan cheese on the side. To really set the mood, add some candlelight!

Pre-cooked shrimp

We 💜 Food!

Like spaghetti, linguine noodles are long and thin, but unlike spaghetti, they are flat instead of round. Traditionally, spaghetti is usually served with meat and tomato dishes, like the romantic dinner in *Lady and the Tramp*. Linguine (pronounced "lin-GWEE-nee") is usually served with seafood or pesto.

Frozen Strawberry Yogurt Dessert

Strawberries are often called the "fruit of love." In ancient Rome, strawberries were associated with Venus, the goddess of love. People took offerings of strawberries to Venus's temples.

An old legend says that if a person eats half a strawberry, then gives the other half to someone they like, the two people will fall in love! So a strawberry recipe is a must to round off your romantic, Valentine's Day dinner.

This delicious frozen yogurt recipe couldn't be simpler to make. Make sure you prepare the dessert the day before you want to eat it, as it needs to be frozen overnight.

We ♥ Food!

Strawberries are a fat-free, super-healthy treat. When you think of eating fruit to get **vitamin C**, you probably think of eating an orange. Strawberries, however, contain more vitamin C (per equal helping) than oranges! Strawberries are also a good source of **fiber**, which keeps our digestive systems working well.

You will need – ingredients:

These quantities will make two servings of dessert

1¾ cups fresh strawberries

7 ounces condensed milk

2 cups low fat Greek yogurt

1 to 2 tablespoons of superfine sugar

You will need – equipment:

Knife

Food processor or blender

Mixing bowl

Wooden spoon

Plastic container with lid, for freezing

Sieve

Small bowl

Plastic wrap

Wineglasses for serving (one per person)

Pieces of red ribbon about 20 inches (51 cm) long
(one to decorate each glass)

Remember to ask an adult for help when you are using the knife, food processor, or blender.

Step-by-Step:

1. Wash the strawberries, remove the stems, and slice each strawberry into about six pieces.

2. Blend half of the strawberries in the food processor or blender, until they are pureed (a thick sauce).

3. Put half of the strawberry puree into the mixing bowl. (Put the other half of the puree to one side to make a pouring sauce later.)

4. Stir the condensed milk into the puree in the mixing bowl. Then gently stir in the yogurt.

5. Fold the chopped strawberries into the mixture. (To fold means to mix very gently rather than stirring.)

6. Scrape the mixture into the freezer container and put on the lid. Put into the freezer overnight or as long as needed to freeze.

7. To make a pouring sauce for your dessert, mix the remaining strawberry puree with the sugar.

8. Pour the sauce through a sieve into a small bowl. Use a spoon to push the sauce through the sieve. Throw away the seeds and lumpy bits left in the sieve.

Strawberry sauce

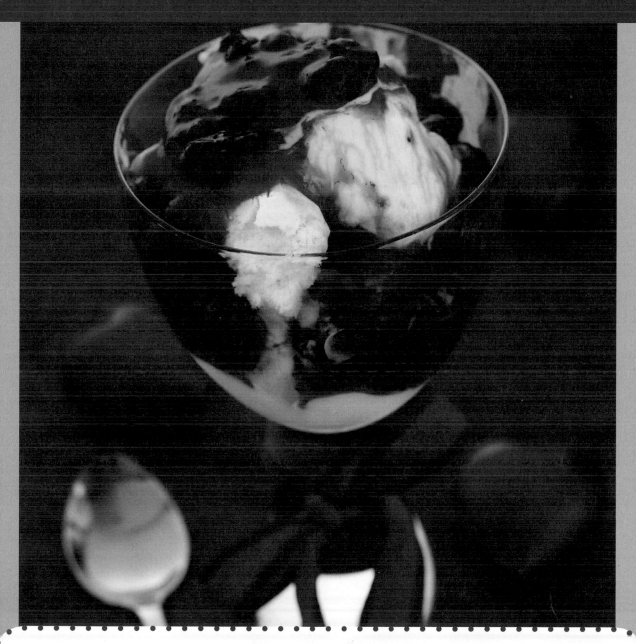

Step-by-Step:

9. Cover the bowl of sauce with plastic wrap and store in the refrigerator until ready to use.

10. Remember to remove the frozen dessert from the freezer 30 minutes before serving to allow it to soften a little.

11. When you're ready to serve, scoop some of the dessert into each wineglass. Drizzle some of the strawberry sauce over the top. Tie a piece of ribbon into a bow around the stem of each glass and serve!

Red Velvet Cupcakes

More than ever, cupcakes are a favorite in cooking magazines and cookbooks. There are even television shows all about cupcakes! Cupcakes are a fun treat for birthday parties and other celebrations, such as Valentine's Day. They're easier to eat than a slice of cake, and you don't even need a plate or a fork! With the red velvet cupcake recipe that follows, you'll be sure to have plenty of admirers on Valentine's Day!

We  Food!

Some of the food coloring we use today comes from natural sources. One of these, called carmine, is a bright-red color that comes from an acid produced by insects known as cochineal insects. Carmine was first used by people in Mexico and Central America to dye clothing.

You will need – ingredients:

These ingredients will make approximately 24 cupcakes

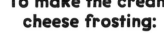

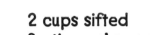

To make the cupcakes:

2½ cups all-purpose flour

1 teaspoon baking powder

1½ cups sugar

1 teaspoon salt

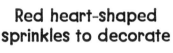

2 teaspoons cocoa powder

1½ cups vegetable oil

1 cup buttermilk (at room temperature)

2 large eggs

2 tablespoons red food coloring

1 teaspoon white distilled vinegar

1 teaspoon vanilla extract

To make the cream cheese frosting:

8 ounce (226 g) package cream cheese, softened

1 stick butter, softened

1 teaspoon vanilla extract

2 cups sifted confectioners' sugar

Red heart-shaped sprinkles to decorate

You will need – equipment:

Cupcake pan

Paper cupcake liners

Medium mixing bowl

Sieve for sifting flour

Large mixing bowl

Electric hand mixer

Wooden spoon

Toothpick

Butter knife

Potholder or oven mitt for handling cupcake pan

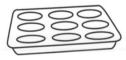

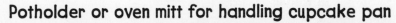

Step-by-Step:

Remember to ask an adult for help when you are using the electric hand mixer and oven.

To make the cupcakes:

1. Preheat the oven to 350°F (175°C).

2. Line the cupcake pan with the paper cupcake liners.

3. In the medium mixing bowl, sift together the flour, baking powder, sugar, salt, and cocoa powder.

4. Put the vegetable oil, buttermilk, eggs, red food coloring, vinegar, and vanilla extract into the large mixing bowl and gently beat together with the electric hand mixer.

5. Add the sifted dry ingredients to the wet ingredients and mix with the wooden spoon until all the ingredients are combined and smooth.

6. Fill each cupcake liner about $^2/_3$ full.

7. Bake for 20–25 minutes, turning the baking pan halfway through. Test to see if they're done by sticking a toothpick into the center of a cupcake. If it comes out clean, your cupcakes are ready to take out of the oven!

8. Allow your cupcakes to cool completely before frosting.

Step-by-Step:

To make the cream cheese frosting:

1. In a large mixing bowl, stir together the cream cheese, butter, and vanilla, then use the electric mixer to beat them together until well blended.

2. Gradually beat in the sugar so it blends with the creamy mixture. Use the mixer on a low speed.

3. Increase the mixer's speed to high and beat until very light and fluffy.

4. Use a knife to smooth lots of frosting onto the top of each cupcake.

5. Decorate the frosting with red heart-shaped sprinkles.

Super Strawberry Slushies

These glamorous, red-colored, healthy drinks are perfect for serving at a Valentine's Day party. You can also make them for your Valentine dinner guest, or guests, before you serve your specially prepared meal. The quantities below will make three small glasses of slushie— one each for your guests, perhaps, and one for the chef!

You will need – ingredients:

To make the slushies:

1 cup whole fresh strawberries

1 cup pink unsweetened grapefruit juice

3 tablespoons superfine sugar

10 ice cubes

To decorate the glasses:

2 tablespoons superfine sugar

2 tablespoons grapefruit juice

3 strawberries

You will need – equipment:

2 or 3 wide rimmed glasses

2 saucers

Food processor or blender

Knife

Cocktail straws (you can cut ordinary straws in half)

Step-by-Step:

Remember to ask an adult for help when you are using the knife and blender.

To decorate the glasses:

1. Put the 2 tablespoons of grapefruit juice in one saucer, and the 2 tablespoons of superfine sugar in the second saucer.

2. Take a glass and dip the rim into the juice. Then dip the rim into the sugar. Repeat with each of the glasses to give them a frosted look.

To make the slushies:

1. Wash and dry the strawberries. Put three small strawberries to one side for decoration (don't remove their stems). Remove the stems from the other strawberries.

2. Put the strawberries, grapefruit juice, and sugar into the food processor or blender. Put on the lid and blend until the mixture is smooth.

3. Now add an ice cube, and blend. Add another ice cube, and blend. Continue to add the ice cubes one by one until the mixture is smooth.

4. Immediately pour into your glasses.

5. Cut a slit into each of the decorative strawberries (about a third of the way into the strawberry). Then slide a strawberry onto the rim of each glass. Add a straw and serve!

Chocolate-Dipped Strawberries

This recipe combines strawberries and chocolate—what could be sweeter or more romantic? Make chocolate-dipped strawberries as a gift for your valentine or as a delicious dessert.

You will need – ingredients:

1 cup semisweet chocolate chips
(or half semisweet chocolate and half white chocolate)

1 carton of strawberries
(12 to 20 strawberries)

Chopped nuts
(for decoration)

Finely shredded coconut
(for decoration)

You will need – equipment:

Paper towels

Cookie sheet

Waxed paper

Small bowl

Spoon

Step-by-Step:

Remember to ask an adult for help when you are using the microwave.

1. Wash the strawberries (don't remove the stems) and dry thoroughly using paper towels. It's very important that the strawberries are dry because the chocolate will not set if it gets wet.

2. Cover the cookie sheet with the waxed paper

3. Put the chocolate chips into the small bowl. Microwave for 30 seconds on high to melt the chocolate. (If you are using two types of chocolate, melt them in separate bowls.)

4. Stir the chocolate. Microwave for another 30 seconds.

5. Stir the chocolate and let the heat of the chocolate melt the lumps. If you still have lumps, microwave for 10 more seconds. Keep stirring and giving the chocolate 10-second blasts in the microwave until it is fully melted and smooth.

6. Hold the strawberries by their stalks and dip into the chocolate. Place on the cookie tray to set.

7. If you wish, sprinkle the strawberries with chopped nuts and finely shredded coconut.

8. If you are giving your chocolate-dipped strawberries as a gift, put them into a pretty box.

31

Glossary

ancient Rome (AYN-shent ROHM) A civilization dating back around 2,700 years ago, centered in the city of Rome that is today the capital of Italy, that grew to become one of the largest empires in the world.

executed (EK-suh-kyoot-ed) Killed, usually as a political act or as punishment for a crime.

feast day (FEEST DAY) A day on which a celebration is held, often to honor a person's birth or death.

fiber (FY-ber) Material in plants that the human body can't break down and that helps move food through our digestive systems.

saint (SAYNT) A person recognized for his or her good deeds and holy nature, usually by a Christian religion.

tradition (truh-DIH-shun) A practice that a group of people have performed for many years and that passes on to the people who come after them.

vitamin C (VY-tuh-min SEE) A substance found in certain foods, especially citrus fruits and green vegetables, that helps the body with many of its functions, including growth, healing, and repair.

Index

C
chocolate, 8, 30
chocolate–dipped strawberries, 30–31
cupcakes, 24

E
easy Valentine's rocky road, 8–11

F
fiber, 20
frozen strawberry yogurt dessert, 20–23

H
hearts, 12

I
I love you cookies, 12–15

L
Lady and the Tramp, 16, 19
love, 4, 12, 20

M
measuring, 7

P
pasta, 16, 19

R
red velvet cupcakes, 24–27

S
safety and hygiene, 6
strawberries, 20, 30
super strawberry slushies, 28–29

T
techniques, 7
ti amo linguine, 16–19

V
Valentine's Day, 4, 8, 24
Venus, 20
vitamin C, 20

Websites

For web resources related to the subject of this book, go to: www.windmillbooks.com/weblinks and select this book's title.